LOBSTER WITH OL' DIRTY BASTARD

"I'm everywhere,
You ain't never there."
—*Jay-Z*

LOBSTER WITH OL' DIRTY BASTARD

Michael Cirelli

Hanging Loose Press
Brooklyn, New York

Published by Hanging Loose Press, 231 Wyckoff Street, Brooklyn, New York 11217. All Rights Reserved. No part of this book may be reproduced without the publisher's written permission, except for brief quotations in reviews.

www.hangingloosepress.com

Printed in the United States of America
10 9 8 7 6 5 4 3 2 1

Hanging Loose Press thanks the Literature Program of the New York State Council on the Arts for a grant in support of the publication of this book.

Cover design by Allison Schlegel
Author photo by Sara Zaidi
Cover photo of Manton Avenue Men's Football Team circa 1978. Number 26 is Michael Cirelli Sr.

Library of Congress Cataloging-in-Publication Data

Cirelli, Michael
     Lobster with ol' dirty bastard / Michael Cirelli.
          p. cm.
     ISBN-13: 978-1-931236-96-6
     ISBN-13: 978-1-931236-95-9 (pbk.)
     I. Title. II. Title: Lobster with ol' dirty bastard.
     PS3603.I74L63 2008
     811'.6--dc22

                                                            2007047337

 Produced at The Print Center, Inc. 225 Varick St., New York, NY 10014, a non-profit facility for literary and arts-related publications. (212) 206-8465

CONTENTS

DYING LIKE A DOG

The hospital pulses like a sewing machine.
Nurses in rubber shoes rap the pedals to keep
the motor going. Got to get every stitch just right.
Aren't the kidneys artful? Shapely as beans, even
when they are dying. Someone brings him another
plate of shrimp. At least he hasn't lost the hunger.
His liver gave out a few days ago, went to bed in all
its dark, reddish-brown beauty. Can you believe
they use the word *lobe* to describe it. That they compare
the largest organ in the body, to a football. Instead,
they should call it the soft triangle inside you, or the fat
boomerang in the belly that makes you always return
to the street corner where you came from,
until finally, you don't.

—Erica Miriam Fabri

I.
3 FEET HIGH & RISING

DAMN IT FEELS GOOD TO BE A GANGSTA

In a sporty version of a Mercedes, a "Baby Benz,"
I sat parked in front of the Chad Brown housing projects
alone in the passenger seat, like an albino fish, for long long
long minutes as young girls with braids and beads and little-boy-men
with scabs on their stomachs tapped the glass—and I pressed down
on the automatic lock button like it was a neck pulse or a safe
word in Braille—and I didn't let go until my father walked out with a chest
made of scales and whistled, with two fingers at the corners of his lips,
to the shadows that responded from a window, while a word or two
(in a dialect coded to my not-wanting-to-know ears) spun through the air
like helicopter seeds and he hopped into the car and handed me
a new pair of Jordans, stashed a sandwich bag under the leather seat
—and before we sped off, made his chubby fingers into a pistol and shot
two of the waving little-boy-men with a smile.

LOBSTER WITH OL' DIRTY BASTARD

The broken-down fishing boats on the docks rock back and forth
as if there is music in the air. **Norma Jean, Captain's Girl, Jenny**, all hips and
bounce—*shimmy shimmy ya* in their slips. Across the street, Randazzo's Clam Bar,
"the pride of Sheepshead Bay," bustles. Inside, not fisherman nor pirate, but rapper
Ol' Dirty Bastard has his own seat, where he reigns with sunglasses and a vinyl bib.
Dirty *likes it raw*, so raw he fathered 13 children, and when he rolls up to Randazzo's,
in his black school bus with 24-inch rims, his clan of offspring pour out like bass.
Mama Randazzo sighs and smiles that forced diagonal smile, as she drags 6 tables together.
There are platters of mussels and little necks with mouths wide open!
Dinner rolls bounce off the walls like handballs! Sword fights break out with shrimp
skewers, the toddlers wear calamari rings on their fingers like diamonds, and lil' Rusty
does the fake-sneeze-trick that leaves an oyster in his open palm. Ol' Dirty is ravishing
a huge boiled lobster, drawn butter dripping down his chin, as he cracks open the claws
with his golden fangs.

VEAL

The calf is lifted from inside his mother
by four robust Italian women
with gloves made of feathers
and brought to a shallow pool
of fine-grained salt
where he is fed from porcelain
bowls—milk and butter and honey—
and is rubbed down with extra virgin
olive oil three times daily
for eighteen weeks
until the priest arrives with his pewter
blade and unlocks the thick
Montepulciano from the calf's neck
like pulp, and hangs him from
an anchor until he is ready
to be wrapped in cotton gauze
and brought to the butcher
for the flesh to be separated
like Eucharists into bowls and saucers and cups
and then offered to the chefs
who pound the meat flat as wax paper,
dip it in powder, cover it in oil and garlic
and mushrooms and artichokes and fire
speaks to it
like a snake,
before my dinner is plated
onto bone-white china
and brought to me sitting with my grandma,
because Pops dropped us off
before he went to run another "errand,"
(like the "errands" to South Providence,
or the "errand" inside the laundromat,
or the one that left me at a rest stop
off I-95 in the middle of nowhere)—

but this "errand" was quick apparently,
because by the time my veal came,
Pops walks through the door
loud as a motorcycle, shakes the hands
of Anthony and Vince and Franco,
pulls up a chair
at our table, takes my plate
and scarfs down my dinner
in three bites,
slurps my Coke from liquid to air
in a gulp,
flags down our waiter
and orders *two more*
veal scaloppinis—
one for me,
and another for him.

BALLOON

*Michael, you can't expect the world from me, when my feet
are hardly on the ground,* she said. And also, *I want to hollow
you out and make a sleeping bag of you.* And again, something
along the lines of, *I feel like a wild bird, perched on you.* One more
time, he wanted to hear, *hold me baby baby baby,* while they rolled
around the bed like cotton candy—He didn't know what
to expect: a levitating lover? a confused camper? turkey vulture?
So he worked on his helium tricks nightly, under a boxcar constellation,
below a nervous cuckoo. He said, *The world is yours, and I made you
grass slippers.* And also, *I've pitched tent for you, on the campus of my bed.*
And again, something along the lines of, *My heart is a birdfeeder. Home.*
One more time, she wanted to hear, *anything for you anything for you
easy,* because that's how she liked her cake—So he whipped up
a balloon, from the blank husk of his body. Aimed it at Puerto Rico.
A silk string around his toe. A head full of motley feathers.
If you're gonna be up there, he said, *hold me baby
baby baby.*

Culture

In Ghana, the women dress in water
colors. In Sierra Leone, the garb is as brazen
as lions. A man in Istanbul stacks 17 saucers
on his head for a hat. Indian girls wear peacocks
for skirts. In Islamic culture, a woman's face shines
from the middle of a black hole.
Hippies bleed tie-dye, Beatniks balance berets,
Hasidim rock full beards with silk ribbons coiling
from their sideburns—but in hip-hop culture, shell toes
scuff the pavement like city crabs. Men hang whole villages
from their necks, and when they smile, the diamonds in the teeth
make the ladies squint—these same ladies in their too-tight jeans
showing off ass, for the fellas
in their too-loose jeans showing off ass.

THE GIVER

When he died, it was said
that he was owed
at least fawty-five grand,
easy. But didn't have a thing
when the last firework
expired, not even a match.

"I'm gonna live by the streets,
and die by the streets,"
he would say,
with his mouth full
of shrimp cocktail,
surrounded by every
tag-a-long-mooch-kiss-ass
in the neighborhood,
taking big bites (on his dime).

His sweatpants hung so low
with rolled-up cash
that it looked like cans of Coke
were in each pocket,
and he'd peel bills
from those fat green wads
and hand them out
like bubblegum.

There were Cadillacs,
Beemers, Cutlasses—
pulling up and away
and money changing directions
like a kite.
I asked no questions
as I looped the fat shoelaces
onto fresh suede Gazelles,
held my pants up

with a shiny belt buckle
bearing his name.

They say money
can't buy love,
but my heart blushed
when I got that remote control
Monster truck.

I grew four new aortas
(like fungi)
the year a surfboard
made of glass
was under the Christmas tree.

In '89, a computer
that covered my whole desk
(way before Google had put
needle and thread to the Internet)
was > a thousand kisses.

When he didn't pick me up
on our Saturday visits
for three months straight,
he wrapped a thick gold watch
around the bruise.

I remember
how my love blew up
like a hot air balloon
as he walked into the Suzuki shop
and bought me a Jet Ski
with a stack of sulfur.

Even now, from the other side
of breath, he's given me
all these thumbtacks
I line up like syllables.

GIVING ME THE GHOSTFACE

He didn't give me the *gas face*. Never shot me the *stink eye*, even on
report card day. No *screw face* either. And certainly not the porcelain saucer
that sat beneath the *mean mug*. I was his namesake, raised by my Middle
Name, and when Saturday mornings came, my mother (with the stench
in her eye), would bark, *Michael Joseph, you're wasting your time!* as I waited
by the window. My Middle Name was out earning the roof for us—
so I waited under the no-roof, with birds in the place of shingles, for a father
called *visitation* to show his teeth. Mother mean mugged me, in need of
a Phillips head, unscrewing her word *deadbeat,* or her other word
dopehead, as the sun drew a full smile across the no-roof, then shut off
the free electricity until the next morning. Again, my father had given me
the ghostface: He put a pantyhose over his skull, and drove that car
that sparkled like anchovies, anywhere but here.

COMMON POSTS UP WILLIE HARPER

Before vegetarian advocacy, Common Sense was a cocky freshman
with NBA-sized shoes to fill. Pre-Nag Champa incense, Lonnie Jr. puffed
a pinner with his boys in the ball closet, before the game. Years prior
to being prefixed "conscious," Junior had a name to live up to, a legacy
that caught him extra elbows. As the Luther South bleachers packed
like peppercorn and fennel in Italian sausage, he laced them Converse
up anyways. Willie Harper was built like a stockcar, 3-time All-State.
Willie had four dashes shaved into his left eyebrow, and an illegible
word tattooed on his forearm. He walked straight up to young Lonnie,
looked down on him, then smirked—exposing a gold-capped tooth.
Before the convoys to Cuba to meet with Assata, Lonnie Jr. tucked his jersey
deep into his red and white shorts. He pivoted his left leg across Willie's
jutting elbow, caught the inbound pass with one hand, his right, then crossed
over to the hoop with his left. He called Willie a *fag* as the ball swished.

LOSING THE TOWEL

My father is a myth. I have a cousin
who talks about him like he has hooves.
Looks up to him like a planet made
of chrome. Everyone in the bar tells me he's
their *favorite.* Somehow he became a golden calf
that I knew only as the sum of his stories.
Never as a man made of flesh and teeth.
Instead, I conjure everyone on Manton Ave
to write his prayers: It was early afternoon
and my father was taking a shower.
The music coming from the downstairs apartment
was loud and black, so loud that the water
in the tub changed tenses. He asked politely once,
then twice, for the first-floor derelicts to turn it down.
He asked a third time and *the white-trash junkies*
gave him lip, so he wrapped a towel around his fat
body, big as a giant beanbag, still dripping,
and ran downstairs—with punches solid as buoys
and curses ripe as roses and blood slicker
than silk—and he lost his towel
and *he's butt-ass-naked in the middle of the street pounding*
the shit outta them dumb fucks, and the rap
was loud as police sirens out the first-floor window,
and his stomach was bouncing up and down
like lovemaking as he punched more and more
until finally he stopped, looked down
at those white-trash junkies with asterisks circling
their heads like mockingbirds
—and he called those dumb fucks *n******.*

WHY KANYE CRASHED

Maybe because the car bucked like a thoroughbred
at the corner of Beverly & Cahuenga—so when the light
turned shamrock, (and with the weightlessness in the head
that money makes), he stomped the gas pedal like a roach
and the blueberry Lexus said *go* and slid like mercury on cold tile
down the road—where the L.A. lights were mobiles
and the helicopters spoke lullabies as they cut the air
like the air was whipped cream and the eyelids were pressed tight
with silver dollars—until the road said *no.*
It was a bad time to dream, with the car spinning like a nickel
directly into the mouth of a bus stop—but I suppose it was a blue
and black melody that must have come to him, a snaggle-toothed verse
that jutted out like a cactus, a metaphor for home that could only
be remembered when his eyes were closed.

RIDE OR DIE

That night, he yanked me like a carrot outta bed,
and put me in the backseat of the Lincoln Continental.

It was some odd hour I had never seen, and Dad
was visibly steam engine, obviously peeved.

I watched his eyes in the rearview mirror, half-awake-
half-asleep, treading the fog of tooth fairies, as he drove.

He was driving so fast that the scenery outside looked stretched
as the sky drained all of the dark from its pores.

What sobered my half-slumber, what killed the buzz of sheep,
was that I noticed Dad's eyelids—

they started to slump, then slouch, then fold inward
like fiddleheads. And I stared hard at that rearview,

—so hard the veins in my head were like roots—

and I tried to will his eyes apart, using my young magic to will
them open *open open*, spelling *abracadabra* over and over with my lips—

When I finally woke up, I was alone in the car, in an empty
parking lot. The pillow under my head leaked one black feather.

Monster

Monster is the newest nickname she's given me.
She said it was a combination of my wolfish beard
and my throat-wrenching claws that drove her to it.
It came to her after the fifth time I left scrapes,
then clumped back to my cave. But I hate monsters,
I told her. *Even Frankenstein*, she asked? I detest
Frankenstein, I sneered. *How about The Abominable
Snowman?* The snowman has bad teeth, I responded.
What about the Hunchback of Notre Dame? That guy,
I said, is always looking at my feet. *But you always wear
nice sneakers*, she replied, as she stepped on my left bigfoot.
Well what about vampires? I especially hate vampires, I told her.
Why's that? she asked. Because I know how they love you,
my dear.

KRS-1 SLEEPS AT PROSPECT PARK

On cold nights, the blue lips of Lord Krishna
would whisper Ralph Waldo Emerson to sleep, and in
Emerson's dreams, words would build a home at the edge
of a deep lake. The fir trees called the names of all the ghosts
of England, and Krishna blew a dagger out the side of a conch—
Many years later, on the Eastern Parkway side of Prospect Park,
where drummers meet on Sundays to subpoena their homelands,
a young KRS-1 eats a Jamaican patty under an elderberry bush.
He writes *Black Cop* on the wax paper. He lies on the ground
where the Battle of Long Island was fought against British soldiers
who never questioned their government. The stars in the sky
are ghosts that he knows are there, and he dreams of the South Bronx
that spit him out like a watermelon seed. Under his head rests
Self-Reliance like a pillow.

THE YEAR OF THE HOT DOG

Last year, in *The Year of the Crossbow*, he pulled back
the sharp arrow of his tongue and annihilated every
posy in the hothouse—having plucked roots from *The Year of
the Apron* when the stains were family silhouettes passed down
through *The Year of Half-Smoked Cigarettes*, and *The Year
of Repossessions*, and the long staircases and dead canaries
from *The Year of the Young American Divorcee*, when he and
Patricia endured *The Year of Rusted Anvils and Broken
Racetracks*, having graduated through *The Year of Finger Paintings*,
The Year of the Penalty Box, and finally *The Year of Unfinished
Years*, after flunking out of spirituality,
and surviving *The Year of Slow Deaths* where every smile
was a guillotine, and that same year seemed to linger like a Buddhist
life cycle, like constant déjà vu, until he dragged his Adidas
through *The Year of Beasts of Burden*, which seemed longer than
most years, longer than twice the ardor in the year before last:
The Year of the Not-Good-Enoughs,
that owns six days in every week still, that made his mouth
a scalpel and supplanted the zucchini blossoms in her chest—
It earned him the nickname Monster from the girl with six flowers
strapped to her hairdo, the girl with hands stronger than a shield, who twisted
them arrows like cherry stems and nudged him into *The Year of the Hot Dog*,
this very year, when *everything is relish,* because he can walk sockless
through the mustard patch and finally remember to thank her
for not giving up on me.

SUGE KNIGHT SET IT UP

*The allegation made…is that both the murders of Biggie and Tupac
were arranged by Death Row Records boss, Suge Knight.—BBC News*

Suge Knight put the bling in my father's eye. At age 5, I was crowned
"King of the Pool," and it was Suge's doing. Suge orchestrated my parents'
divorce, got me an honest stepdad to throw a baseball at. In 1993, I graduated
Summa Cum Laude, and he set the whole thing up from his small two-bedroom
in Compton. Or the internship in Poland, where I met Kasia, with a tongue like
a mosquito—Suge was my black Santa Claus. I fell in love with every girl who ate
pistachios from my red palm, and Suge watered the pistachio trees. But as I got older,
Suge wasn't so sweet. Suge made Lisa leave me, had Marni move away while I
was in Texas. I wore a headache—like a fitted cap—for 9 months, and he embroidered
its logo. He licked the stamps on rejection letters. Put the glitch in my Trojan.
From a hot jail cell in Nevada, he painted the line blue, and he even pushed the car
to Planned Parenthood—as all the shells in me were crushed to white powder.
Suge Knight sent the FBI crashing through my father's door, where he was wolfing
down a chicken parm like it was his last meal on Earth.

II.
THE HEADPHONE MASTERPIECE

CODY CHESNUTT PLAYS GOD

They say he's a Born Again now, a far cry
from the *bitch I'm broke* days. His cape
is embroidered with gold crosses and his
short, tight Afro is the shape of a black halo.
I think God put onyx marbles into his eyes,
made him look like a blind man.
He unzips the chords of his guitar like the zipper
on a down pillow. Feathers fall out onto the crowd
and all of us stare as if we are watching a campfire.
The feedback crackles.

PUNK ROCK PLATH

I attribute
it to you and your punk

rock garden, the collections
of stingers and pollen

from the gully arms
of azaleas like so many patches

on dirty hoodies. Your lips
are steel-toed rusted roof.

The rift between you
and them pre-Sid and slang

on the hooved motorcycle
you straddled like a loaded

word was an articulate eff
off Mr. Parliament.

Oh Sylvie,
we didn't need that music then.

No one wanted you
to prove your metaphors.

But you did, with leather skin
and eyes like spikes you left us,

a gallop into your myth
that set like Jello each night.

This is for teaching us how
to chug hot air with no flinch.

This is for distortion made sweet.

DEAD ASS

In the bodega, a young girl wearing
jeans so tight she has to use turpentine
to get them off, says to her friends,
Damn, it's dead ass raining out!

I was enamored. Instead of cats and dogs,
I pictured donkey corpses falling from
the sky, clogging the gutters.
That's some "serious" rain.

The song on the radio said that the po-po was:
"tryna catch me ridin' dirty." I imagined
Chamillionaire wearing a 20 lb. gold chain
with mud dripping off Jesus's shiny toes,
Krayzie Bone in four-hundred-dollar jeans,
with grass stains on the knees.

In Oakland, the sound there is "hyphy." To me,
that alien word means gooney-goo-goo.
To me, that word is my dead father's kiss.
But to thousands of youngsters whose trousers sink
below the Plimsoll line of their asses, hyphy
music makes their bodies dip up and down
like oil drills.

These words make me feel old, and alabaster.
When I hear something new, it's like I discovered it
for the first time, like I excavated it from the mouth
of a teenager. So I dust it off with my fossil brush
and try to jam it into the keyhole of academia.

I am not afraid of dope lyrics, not dope meaning weed
but dope meaning good. My kind uses scrilla to board
up the windows of shook.

Fo' shizzle, crunk, hella: I place in glass jars like rare moths.
I want to hang them on the doors of sonnets
like a welcome sign to an apartment
I don't live in.

DEAREST WORKSHOP

I'm sorry if my poem
hit you over the head today.

I was trying to beef it up,
give it more punch and

apparently the ending got
away from me, wiggled

off the line like a feisty rainbow
trout. But it was just humiliating

last week limping through school
with that giant shiner around

my left eye. All week I worked
my abstract, pumped irony, stayed

up late praying to my avant-guardian
angel, burned incense to Ashbery—

and after all that, my sentences are still
flat. It seems I've busted my index

finger in a word playground, the loaded pun
shot blanks into my foot, carnal syntax

got the best of me. Porno and Play Station
has sucked the milk from my days.

But this week, I promise to lock myself
in a stanza and throw away the keyboard

until I stink so damn good you'll say
I wouldn't change a thing.

Welcome to my sauna where everyone
speaks *peanuts here!* This is where

I rub turtle wax all over my verses
until they are more polished than my

grandpa's Town Car. I want you
to see yourself in them.

LOSING CREATIVITY

I have become so absorbed by my job
that I go to bed rapt in it only to

wake up the next morning
and do it. It seems that good benefits

have squelched good metaphors, and that's
the best I can come up with.

Try this:

I stare at a keyboard where the letters are out of order.

I try to unlock that keyboard like it's a safe
filled with paper coins.

I speak Dollar-Sign-Language.

I drink coffee. Make talk shrink.

There is no room for simile here.
I am like … a poet who's forgotten how to make one.

So I'm losing creativity, I say to the closing teeth
of the elevator.

I remember when I won the gold key
for my watercolor in middle school.

By 9th grade I wanted to pursue
a career in pole vaulting. I loved

getting high. But who's to say I still can't
paint: *Still Life of Poet Emailing*.

Who's to say I can't make something of this
poem yet.

We don't lose creativity, we squander
our time.

I used to rub on these letters for hours
until they shined like patent leather shoes.

We talk about our "gifts" like they're something
we're born with

but my painting had so many layers
of watercolor that the paper warped—

Inside my chest
is a tiny box wrapped in
snowman wrapping paper,
with a big silver bow on top.

Inside the box is a fang covered in gold.

I worked hard
for that metaphor.

CROSSING BROOKLYN BRIDGE

to Walt Whitman

I too have gawked
in awe at the undeniable
skyline—the bridges that
hyphenate the boroughs.

I too am a comrade of chafed
boots and soiled aprons, in fellowship
with the rough pronunciation
of the multitudes.

I can see you are a fan of close
quarters and clanking elbows,
portly pigeons putt putting down
the avenues.

But this gets old in New York,
and I want my space—to open
my newspaper like a Yao Ming wingspan,
deep in the throat of the *F* train's gutter mouth.

I'm a fan of Ansel Adams's
calendars and Disney's Epcot Center,
the clean versions of civilization's major
cities where everyone understands *hot dogs!*

I can only feel like you Walt, when I rush
down the long glossy corridors
of The Garden, the hundreds and hundreds
stacked in public assembly—

As the flood tide of excitement
lifts us out of our narrow seats, tiny bodies
oscillate on hard wood, and the game
clock blares like a fog horn.

New York City Is Loud

When I first heard Her
raucous sneeze that was a sneeze
times forty-four
I was so aghast that I didn't bless Her.
She is loud as a gazillion pigeons
making baby pigeons, loud as a wrecking ball
being pulled towards the sky-
scrapers. Louder than skyscraper fingernails,
on the sky. Train hooves clack & cap
guns clap. Big lips smack & jackhammers
jack. Call it clacking, clapping, smacking
or jacking, I call it loud. The police sirens
scream like a phone call
at 4 am to explain
how the last drop of air clicked away
from your father. Between the contraption
and the voices on the ends, telephones
elicit noise exuding noise. When someone
is hollering
yo yo yo from behind, don't look back.
The garbage can is a rip-roaring fellow.
The ice cream truck is decibels.
A Chevy is bassing *smack that oh*
smack that, down Ocean Ave.
There is a body that was a man curled
around the foot of a dumpster, and another
man on his cell phone is nudging him
with his glassy leather shoe. The nudge
sounds like kicking a tin can.
One baby rat squeaking + a baker pulling
bread from an oven + the school bell at PS 132 + *ching*
of the cash register + the butcher knife's *plonck,*
all inhabit the symphony of loud.
Dollar Vans honk for dollars,

and dollar-honking is the loudest type
of honking.
After a day of loud—when I want
nothing more than the silence of lemons,
the whisper of face soap, I come home to my lady
who is frying pakora (the oil pops
like firecrackers)—we eat until we are full,
go into our quiet bedroom
and make loud all night long.

DANCING WITH TURTLE

"There are secrets we don't know," she whispered on the dance floor,
where we were spinning like Sufis, her arms raised high above
the turquoise, hips going in and out like a water pump. She had me
shell-shocked. We danced incestuously to Michael *and* Janet that night.
Lionel Richie had us upside down. Hands flapped like flags to *Player's Anthem,*
as I rocked my Frankenstein 2-step. When *Holla Back Girl* marched straight out
them speakers, everyone in the circle bugged out. Flip-flops were dancing shoes.
Big brown clodhoppers—dancing shoes. Penny loafers were dancing shoes.
How could the rhythm hit 'em like this? "There are secrets we don't know,"
Turtle whispered back. The girl with Flashdance hair was exercise in motion.
The dude in all the starch was penguin in motion. I was *tin-roof-rusted*
in motion, and Turtle was Galapagos, snapper, poetry, in motion. Prince's *Kiss*
brought it up a notch, then the mix got wicked as *Poison* lifted everyone off their
booty. There were porpoises gyrating to the left of me, serpents to the right
with breasts like stress balls. The seagull who brushed my right fin tried to
fashion her eyes like hooks, but Turtle was like *Candy*, and I was stuck
on her hard, sweet secret.

"SLAYER"

The night was so thick, the subway so
quiet, I even caught the city nodding off.
My headphones were pulsing on my skull,
the sweet jelly of De La Soul, and I noticed
on the window of the A train that someone
had scratched "Slayer," in the exact font
of the heavy metal band, strewn among
the more narcissistic renditions of graffiti.
I remembered the bathroom stall at my office
that read **AC/DC** in fat green marker on the mirror.
George Coombs even has "Def Leopard" tattooed
onto his forearm. But I've never seen any rapper's
name scribbled by an avid fan. I doubt anyone
has ever written *Queen Latifah Rules!* onto the chest
of a subway door. No "Run DMC" or "Jay-Z" inked
into the skin with pride. As the train kept beating
from stop to stop, closer to home, I held my keys
in my hands nervously. Before I got off, I carved
LUPE FIASCO into the cold, hard glass.

THE MESSAGE

Malcolm was fed 16 bullets because of his. A slug kissed
the jaw of King Jr. and silenced him forever. Gandhi shriveled
like snakeskin. Joan of Arc became Joan of Ash—
So you can understand why Melle Mel was jittery scribbling it
all down, on a napkin, at Lucky's Noodle Shop in Harlem.
Sweat pearled into his green tea. He thought of Jesus
hanging from that dull wood. Heard about the poet Lorca
under an olive tree, shot in the back. Everyone has felt this way though,
he thought. Never could he have imagined what would happen
when he pressed his thumbprint into vinyl. Hip-hop was still
a tadpole. The DJ had just learned to scratch a record and make sounds
no ear had ever conjugated. How was he to know Tupac & Biggie
would follow his lead and get plugged with lead? So he wrote it down,
in big curling letters, emphatic: *don't push me.*

When Talib Kweli Gets Expelled from Brooklyn Tech

He doesn't slam Principal Grabowski's door like a gavel.
He doesn't put on his Yankees hat, in defiance. No middle finger
to the security guard or loogie on the glossy tile. He walks,
his head not high nor slouched, down the corridor and not one
student points or cackles like a hyena. Jon Taylor inserts text
into his ear, beneath the pitch of the bell—as they exchange
ancient Kemetic handshakes—and move on.
Under Ms. Browne's door, he slips his book report like an oil spill.
He shakes the physics teacher's hand firm as apples. He winks
a rainbow at Secretary Ignatius Butler, and opens those heavy blue doors
one last time. It is fall. Winter is showing its baby teeth and the sun
is carrying two hundred spindles of saffron to Florida. The leaves
are like cinder footprints leading to Ft. Green Park. He sits beneath
an oak tree, pulls the book from his backpack, and starts reading again, *Beloved.*

PROFESSOR ALIM WRITES ON PHAROAHE MONCH

Professor writes words like *multirhyme matrix, vast corpus, academic discourse* on the hands of the rapper like henna. Pharoahe's cornrows are *highly intertextual* and *multilayered,* as he sips a shot of wheat grass. But *God's-Gift-to-Vocabulary* isn't impressed when they wrap the *Journal of English Linguistics* (Vol. 31, No. 1) around his tongue like gold gauze. Instead, Monch puts his ear to the brownstone, to hear what twenty knuckled-up kids have to say at the Teen Poetry Slam. The Professor shuffles behind like a butler, filing patents on the *inventive linguistic landscape* of the teenagers. Alim notes how the pH level of Pharoahe's face changes after a thirteen-year-old girl's poem spoke about pain, the way shamans speak of water. He writes *sociolinguistics* across the rapper's throat when no one is looking. Alim whispers *cultural capital* into Pharoahe's ear as the Muslim girl dressed in pure black recited "Gutted Fish." After Tyrone, big as two houses, explained the unbearable lightness of weight, Alim drew a circle around Pharoahe's smile and hollered *ethnographic fieldwork!!* When the rapper clapped loudest for the girl who likened Jesus to *a motherfuckin' poet,* Alim converted to Christianity.

Revolution Concerts

At the concert for revolution, the verses
were sharp as Eldridge Cleaver's, and everyone
pronounced Cuba, *koo-ba*. Three blonde girls
grinded their asses—flat as Novocain—down the leg
of the man with red lips tattooed on his neck,
and the Pakistani kids with umbrellalike hats
kept calling each other the n-word. The freedom
fighter spoke about disarming armored trucks
and freeing all the guns in them (guns being money),
while a young atheist with a T-shirt long as a sundress
hollered *you owe me twenty dollars!* Drunk off Molotov
cocktails, the frat boys turned pit bull, and when the emcees
told everyone to *throw a fist in the air,* I being the non-
conformist that I am, folded my arms into a bow.

YOU WERE WEARING

after Kenneth Koch

You were wearing your Full Moon on the Cusp
of a Bubble Butt jeans, that were waning into your hind
quadrant. Some call them Eve Ensler Bottoms because of
the Granny Smiths on the back pockets, but I call them
Full Moon on the Cusp of a Bubble Butt for obvious reasons.
You said, after you pulled your tongue from my mouth
like a cork, *You make me dizzy.* You were my Moon-Eyed-Girl,
with Dime Piece high heels covering your Honey Dipped
toenails. I had a Fresh To Death crew cut, a Big Papi chain
that glowed like a satellite, and I hollered, *You make a wino of me!*
We chugged our 50 Cent Cabernet, (the rapper not the price),
on a green bench in the Christopher Walken, King of NY, park.
I was feeling intrepid, with Alfred Hitchcock, Hollywood Walk of Fame
stars in my eyes, so I whispered to the Moon, *Let's get dizzy forever....*

THE BEST USE FOR MY POEMS

for Holden

At the poetry reading, no one got my Sierra Leone
reference. No one sympathetic to the crush
of crows on my shoulders. Not a smirk in the direction
of my sonnets about Monster. No *ooh* or *uuhhmp*
for the simile about her, and berries. Not a soul appreciated
the syntax involved with *the turquoise of a turtle's
belly*. Then, a polite clap like a reluctant breeze, and I was back
on the sideline, with my three-year-old nephew, and a stack
of poems curled tight. He picked up those papers, the long white
cylinder of my unmoving words, and held it to his mouth
like a mic, and lip-synced some tongue I was too old to
remember. He took it next, a billy club, and whacked a woman
awake. Then it became a baton he wagged back and forth till
it blurred. Soon the roll of paper was a telescope. As it opened
more on one end, a bullhorn, a little more, a pylon, and the best use—
a dunce cap.

III.
THE LOVE BELOW

CIGARETTE LOVE

I've been in Orchid Love. Been broke over Alexander Hamilton
Love. There was Eyelash Love that had me whipped. I remember
Trainwreck Love, and Getting-Love-While-Driving Love, and Candy Love—
that no matter how sweet, usually dissolved into a sharp tooth, then left
a cavity. How about Hurricane Love that had us clutching palm trees,
pogoing in the wind? Hurray for Buffet Love that left me naked, stuffed,
and exhausted as a panda. Whoop whoop for Police Love that got me cuffed
to a bamboo bedpost. Can't forget First Love and all its sloppy kisses.
First Love that parked behind Stop & Shop every morning before school
and painted my car's windows the deepest shade of fog. There was Come-
Follow-Me Love that had me renovate the scenery in my poems
just to be near it. Landed me in Shreveport Louisiana petrified of crawfish.
There's The More Loving One Love and The More Better Lover Love.
There was love made of 14 lines, or Sonnet Love; there was love made of
too many lines, that Epic Love, not to be confused with Cigarette Love,
(one of the most common loves). Cigarette Love and its slow drag, nearly
impossible to give up the longer it drags on—no matter how many forests
it's capsized. I've had B-Complex Love, and Green Tea Love, and 20-Minutes-
A-Day-Of-Cardio Love, that all lead me to love the reflection
in that aquamarine shell: Holy Turtle Love! Turtle Love that takes its home
everywhere. And it beats. It beats all other love.

KISSING TURTLES

There are those who get off
by putting their heads into the mouths
of alligators, or lions. A Paiute Indian is initiated
by sneaking up on a grizzly and smacking it
on the ass. In Key West, fishermen try to snatch
barracudas out of the ocean with their bare hands.
There is a man in New Zealand that rides
on the backs of ostriches, and a woman
in Calcutta who plucks the venom from cobras
with her fingers. But I've taken to kissing turtles.
First I paint a bright red arrow on her front door.
I turn the switch on my legs to *slowmo*.
I hang a rabbit's foot from my ear for good luck
and rev the purple motor of my tongue
like a juicer. When a turtle comes out for the kissing,
she is soft as bubblegum, smooth as ribbon.
She repeats her one word over and over: *welcome*
welcome, welcome welcome welcome

FRECKLES

I said they're like strawberry
seeds all over her face, like when
she was born her mother rubbed
her cheeks with them. She said
she didn't get that metaphor. So
I said, after counting 100 hundred
of them, that her face is capacious.
She didn't know that word, but liked
the rhyme. I decided to talk about
the dimples on her lower back. She said
everyone has them, and I said *only the sexy
girls,* and how I wanted to take out
my eyeball and rest it in there, cornea
down.

Dear Jack,

You have my favorite girl
all up in a tizzy. She cried

when she heard how your father
died, how he fell from the window—

when *you* were the one born
         with all the feathers.

But that was just the beginning.
Your life read like a motorcade

of hearses, and she soaked every
page till they tore.

She marveled at how easy you
slept through it all. In Greece,

on the stone wall as crows
nibbled your heart, or in Paris

on a bench, when rats with berets
did the same. Love never rested well

with her Mr. Gilbert, so she stays up
all night, with a flashlight, savoring you.

But I have to say: she'll give you a run
for your money Jack. She still feels the sweat

from her first crush behind her ears.
Under her mattress, she keeps every sun-dried

kiss. Forgive me for saying this sir, but I know
for certain—if grief were a cardboard box

filled with charcoal, she could carry that thing
on her back, just as far as you.

GRAFFITI

When Mike tagged "Danielle I
Luv You" in bold blue across the portico
of the 71st St. station on the W Line,

he signed his name and then sprayed
an exclamation point after it: "Mike!"
It is obvious by the size of his

letters, the length that he went to
show his "Luv," that this
is an exclamatory statement.

I can imagine his feeling—
the vapors ricocheting in his head,
fingers tingling with blue pulse

as he hops the empty W and swings
from the hand bars like a motherless school
boy, his scream setting on faded

plywood. Maybe he calls Danielle
from a payphone a stop away,
says, "Dani," (he likes to call her that),

"Meet me at 71st street,
I have a surprise for you." And Danielle,
knowing what sort of surprises

Mike stores in Krylon cans and splattered
knapsacks, feels the strange buzz
of anticipation and fear because

last time Mike survived only 3 letters,
"DAN," before nightsticks burned more
than 3rd rails. His hand is still numb.

I too go to great lengths to convey
this sentiment to my girl,
scrutinizing over colors to say

it in, dodging the mundane that patrols
my language and executing the charges
that make words electric—

When maybe my poem should be:
"Erin I Luv You, Mike!"

SHER-HOLDER

It is the time of year when the trees
look like pumpkins and the pumpkins have
teeth. They are both all lit up. In the park,
they talk about poetry. She explains: *In Pakistan,*
the elders sit around and recite verses to each other.
He aims for a laugh: *In Rhode Island,* he says, *my family*
sits around a table of antipasto playing poker for pennies.
She continues: *When they like the verse, they go 'va*
va va va.' He replies: *In San Francisco, when they like the verse,*
they snap their fingers. On the trail, they crush
twigs under their heels. In bed, they rub their bodies
together like two wires, but instead of making love,
they make fire. The birds high up are like circling silver
dollars. *The verses are called shers,* she said, *pronounced*
"shares." He was thinking about Khadija. *I told my parents*
about you, she said. She loves how he navigates words
like this: gives trees teeth. Last night, after fire-making,
he read her thirty-two Rumi poems. They lay on their backs
and said a prayer. He asked, *I wonder which God will hear this?*
Today he says, *I am your sher-holder.*

LOVE SONG FOR KELIS

I can't compare your voice
to Sarah Vaughn's

sassy tabernacle,
or to Ella's frantic sidestep

up a fire escape on a sticky
night in Chocolate City,

not even to the impenetrable
vaults in Holiday's lungs,

or Nina Simone's sad
peach, with a crew cut.

Your voice is not hash smoke
swirling around an antique fan

in Amsterdam, or the strong finger
of bourbon on my chest,

or Tina Turner's electric
hairdo. It may be simply

the best baby, but it is still
nothing like Chaka Khan's

bottom lip after lovemaking—
I can see how some might think

that your voice is the milky
cherry drowning at the bottom

of a Harlem shake, or that
holding your CD next to my face

in the mirror is the picture
of a perfect couple. And I know

your husband's father is a mediocre jazz great,
but my dad is a cook, ringing bells

when eggs are hot. (I will use
this against you if ever I get a chance.)

I know your voice is sugar
honey iced tea with a striped straw,

and though I may never get a sip, even so,
it still makes my body go *yeah yeah.*

GIRLS, GIRLS, GIRLS

They stroll downtown with petite puppies
hanging on their shoulders like chips.
Tie their hair up into fists and I love them.
On 2nd Ave in black tights and sports bras and
diamonds of sweat across the foreheads. On Grand
Concourse with slick eyebrows. In Harlem
with shoes and purse and belt and earrings
in corroboration with pink. On the Q train wearing a novel
four inches think, on the M15 two babies deep
so her breasts have been yanked down like the *next-*
stop-cord and I love them all nonchalant in their
holsters, (the breasts). I love them on Park Ave with rhinestone
cell phones kissing their ears and I have no problem
in SoHo where their wardrobes cost more than I make
in a year. I love the high heels that hoist the rump into
a half-heart silhouette. I love them pushing strollers,
with tattoos of ships on their shoulders.
On Avenue A with organic apples, at Fordham
with math books, the New School with *Lunch Poems,*
or NYU looking down the library's doomed balcony
wondering; and I love how her glasses slip down the perfect slope
of nose and she keeps pushing them up the way teenage boys
on Flatbush pull up their too-loose jeans. On Dekalb two mothers
swing their daughter like a jump rope! On Mulberry pink tongues from
Syria, South Africa, Singapore, all speak fettuccini alfredo!
On 89th she takes orders with lips shinier than a little red Corvette!
In Far Rockaway they speak! In Washington Heights they voice
lovely! I love them in headwrap, in floss, in sari, in cliché
T-shirts on Houston, on Bowery, with braids that wind
like DNA. I love how the ass moves up and down when they walk
like two fat kids on a seesaw. I love the hard turquoise shell they bloom,
to shield them from boys like me—and despite
it all—still stay soft inside
like Blow Pops.

EMBRACE

On the day of the Embrace, the subway car
was packed as a pill bottle. Each bend of the tracks
forced *touch* between the anxious passengers.
The advertisement above the door had an airbrushed
picture of the actor Jerry Orbach, and urged us
to consider eye donation—as he had, postmortem.
Some people were moved, and others spooked by the idea
of those old showbiz eyes stuffed into the skull
of a little Asian girl. The train kept filling like the downside
of an hourglass. It started slowly:
two stranger fists touched on the handrail, then cautiously,
pinky fingers crept over one another—interlocked.
Then, a black hand, enveloped a white one.
Next, a Hasid hooked his fingers through the belt loop
of some hip-hop jeans. Finally, Puerto Rican sisters
on their way to Hunter College, locked arms with a banker
like monkeys in a barrel. No one was startled, nothing was sexual.
As the momentum shifted more, an elderly woman
took the glasses right off a young man's face, and softly rubbed
her hands all over his nose, lips, ears.
Strangers looked each other in the eyes, deeply.
They held each other, not the poles, as the train rocked along its tracks.

IV.

How astonishing it is that language can almost mean,
and frightening that it does not quite.

—Jack Gilbert

MAKING POEMS

The boy obsesses over his tiny ship.
Changes his mind every time it is ready
to set sail into its bottle. He gets out
of bed early, with a new color on his mind.
Now he paints the hull, gold. He adds a fishing
net and shaves flecks of silver off
an anchovy, to fill it. For the mast, he carves
a Siren out of a toothpick, glues her
to the bow with his spit. He makes
cannonballs from a chip of charcoal.
When he collapses the sails to squeeze
his ship through the small mouth
of the bottle, he notices the fabric
he chose for them—decides they should be velvet.
It goes on and on like this for the boy, who never
launches his ship, never corks the bottle.

Buy You a Train

My mother picked me up
at the bus station in her brand new
Cadillac, shiny and white as a cue ball,
and if anyone deserves that piece
of metal and paint and rubber—it is her,
because I'm sure she bought it with stacks
of nickels and mugs of coffee served,
and she came to pick up her only
son, who *doesn't visit enough,* and the inside
smelled like new footballs
and she smiled large for the car,
but mostly for me, her pride and joy
who *needs to visit more,* and she cranks
the volume of the stereo, *more complicated*
than income taxes, for her only son
who she had when she was seventeen,
who is *better than a diploma,* and who lives
only three hours away and likes *this stuff,*
because the song that was playing on the radio
was black music, and the man
who was singing called himself *T-Pain,*
and his voice was synthesized and reworked
like metal and paint and rubber
until the words spilled out of the speakers
like hot coffee and my mother
liked the song, liked it when he said
I will buy you a train
and she liked the electro-trill in his voice—
and I didn't interrupt her
to tell her he wasn't actually saying *train*—
because she liked how the sound
was *brand new*
coming out of her *brand new car*
with speakers that looked like flies' eyes,

and she picked her only son
up from the bus station, the son
she carried down three flights of stairs
on Leah St. with no car and nowhere
to go when he was just a baby,
and I'm all beard and snot and words now,
and she don't know or need to know all that,
but she likes *this song*
and I chuckle inside because the song
isn't about a train at all—
but my mother, in her shiny white car
that slides like escargot,
is with her little-boy-grown
who *never visits enough* but is here now,
and she is smiling large for the song,
but mostly for me, and I think,
Ma, I *will* buy you a train,
you deserve it, a choo choo for you,
and you can use it
to come visit
anytime you want.

V.
STAKES IS HIGH

Beat to Print

I shoulda seen it coming. The runs to every corner
of "The Ocean State" at every hour of night, the money
that seesawed like tides. As I pounded these letters
so much they disappeared, (my keyboard is all blank
squares), he was making moves on *The Providence Journal*.
As I flew my poems all over the country, people were taking notice
of *him*. People in uniforms to boot! I resented my father
after he got arrested. His name, *my name,* was all over the papers.

CHRISTOPHER WALLACE'S DREAM DEFFERED

The boy would flip through the glowing pages of magazines
and imagine himself pouring champagne over his cereal, wrapping
a mink around his mother's shoulder like an arm. He'd play
his cassette in the boom box so much that his dog would bark
duh-ha duh-ha over and over till the neighbors called the cops.
Sometimes the glint in the sardines reminded him of diamonds,
or stars. Sometimes when he'd sing along with the radio,
he imagined himself on stage—squeezing every last drop out of the lime-
light. On X-mas there was no tree. For birthdays, he was the only one
singing—louder and louder until one day, his voice went hoarse as burnt toast,
dry as a raisin. The boy who'd *never amount to nothin'* dropped out
of high school. He slung on the corner each night, wearing a red
and black lumberjack jacket, with a hat to match. The police sirens
twirled like new galaxies, spun like tiny explosions as the cuffs bit hard.

IT AIN'T ALL GOOD

That morning, when we walked up to
his car (to take me back to Ma's house),
the windows were busted
into a dozen interpretations
of *hurricane*—the tires had scissor-holes
all over their rubber lips, and I was too
Little League to put it all together, or so I
lead on—because the night before
as I lay deep in the molars
of Dad's leather couch I watched him
clean ferociously like he always did,
how he'd Windex the spotless glass
coffee table that no one was allowed to put
anything on anyways, and he'd vacuum
the carpet like he was trying to erase
any dirty word that may have dropped
to the floor, or the motion he used
when he'd scrub the inside of the fridge
that gripped nothing but red cans
of Coke, and then he'd go to the window
and do a scissor-motion
with his fingers, opening and closing
a slot in the blinds and peeking three stories
down to the street
until he returned to the Ajax and the polish
—a wooden case full of porcelain dolls,
a twenty-jet Jacuzzi, each triangle of corner or door
jamb, a TV screen big as a window—and then
back to the scissor hands
and the wink of the blinds, and back
to the immaculate room, and again the fingers
inserted between the blinds
as if into a trigger hole, and then back
to the apartment that never seemed
to be clean enough.

MY HEART IS A BUSTED SECRET SPILLING WITH PROMISE

After we did the freaky deaky,
in the room that had just become
the smartest room in Brooklyn,
we lay on our backs and looked up
at the brain constellation on the ceiling:
medulla oblongata dripping from the curtains.
Beyoncé Knowles never knew our one thing.
Marie Antoinette's soft pouch of a belly
hadn't kneaded this secret. Clarence 13X
never felt this particular this. Outside this door
remains oblivious to behind this door,
where something I said is hidden on the first page
of a book I gave you. Outside this door, your friends
with good teeth have no idea about the shape
I conjure from your mouth. We sit with them and sip
vodka sodas. We sit and talk about movies
and they have no inkling of what it means
when I clamp your upper thigh like some part
of a machine that turns the lids onto jars
of pickles. They know about us, but don't.
The girlfriends of yours know about my serrated edges.
The girlfriends of yours hear the defense witness
that you tuck in your big leather purse. Sometimes
they think 'how romantic.' Sometimes I am a monster.
Behind this door, in the smartest room I made for you,
in my eye you see a city of mosques and temples
built from dazzling blue tiles. Outside the gates
of my mouth, I'm hugging the rubble of our township
so you stay.

PHIFE DAWG AWAITS A KIDNEY

and his mother is patient as an olive tree. She understands
the thick accent of dialysis, isn't fooled by the organ's rhetoric.
Instead, she marvels at the fluid that scrubs her son's blood clean—
makes metaphors about this science-water. She is a poet too, first.
When he was a child she'd belt out Braithwaite verses, as she slipped
insulin into his reluctant arm. Now, she watches as the catheter is prepared
for the funky diabetic, who is thirsty. It enters like his first kiss, from Janet Wilkinson,
under a black moon, on Linden Boulevard, represent represent. Chemistry moves
in his stomach like venom. For a moment he feels like he is going to die.
He wishes some god would roll up in a white Escalade, stick his fist out the window
to drop a shiny new kidney into his palm, as a husky voice booms, *It's all good Diggy*.
His mother sits beside him on the bed, studying each name on her list meticulously.
She is walking along every branch of their family tree—further and further out
onto each limb, trying to find a match in the leaves.

FRAMING THE PICTURE

In the poem, the prepositional phrase
in the kitchen, puts the words *see you later*
into a context. The context becomes the bell.
In the hospital, I watched
my father cry out for his mother,
who has a prosthetic leg. The nuns brought in
silver chains with archangels dangling from them,
and they draped the metal like garlands around his neck.
In the poem, the simile is the one palm that holds
the other in prayer. In the picture, we were zero
words. Next to the radiator, below the window,
I slept most Saturday mornings, waiting
for the car that shined like a new spigot,
to pull up—until Ma dragged me to kindergarten
on Monday. Again and again, I add these
embellishments like a straw hat or handkerchief,
before leaving the house. At the restaurant,
we ate our last meal together on earth. He was
propped on the chair like a whale and devoured
two crème brulees. A poem about poetry is like
an overdeveloped photograph. In the restaurant,
he rubbed his belly like a magic ball as the other customers
stared and slurped oysters. On the street, the pigeons
gave me a simile for a dandelion clock when they puffed
their turquoise necks. I feel this way often. In the poem,
I made love sound better than mercy. In most poems, he is a caricature
of himself. In the kitchen my ears were ringing, I said *see you later*,
not knowing I was lying. The day my father died, the father
who raised me called to rain the news.

ZEV LOVE X LIVE AT HIS BROTHER'S FUNERAL

That day, Zev Love X woke up at five in the morning, hung
over. His brother, Subroc, didn't die like most rappers.
The torso hadn't swallowed five bullets, like multivitamins.
He wasn't cardiac arrested, or suffocated under the down pillow
of addiction. No in-and-out-smash-and-grab that left him
on the studio floor in a mosaic of broken glass. No AIDS,
no shank splicing his intestines like cables. No martyrdom.
Crossing Eastern Parkway, without controversy, sipping
a ginger beer, an '86 Corolla took him out—quick and painless.
What leaves the body dug a hole in the cloudless Brooklyn sky.
Zev picked a black Polo from his hamper, hung it in a hot shower
as steam coaxed the wrinkles out. He placed one red rose on the hood
of the casket and cried for the last time in his life. From that day on,
he wore a metal mask—renamed himself MF Doom.

LIVES OF ASTRONAUTS

He'd been selling drugs so long
that when he got caught he cried snowflakes.

For the next four years (awaiting trial) he dumped
liquor over his head until his kidney floated up

to his throat. In the hospital bed, I poured
powder on his balls that had swollen to the size

of grapefruits. I held the bedpan as he peed
thick composites of burgundy, hoping for yellow.

I hadn't been home in six months and it was hard
not to hold my father accountable for this—

as his organs held him accountable for vodka,
and the FBI held him accountable for cocaine.

That last week he slept in his childhood bed.
Each morning he ate seventeen tiny capsules for breakfast

and wedged his bloated body behind the wheel
of Grandma's Honda to drive to the beach.

He walked across the sand slow like a robot in need
of oil, and stood calf-deep in the ocean, facing the horizon

like a wooden Siren carved into the front of a pirate ship,
as toddlers played tag with the incoming surf.

We all want to die an ordinary death, but want to live
the lives of astronauts. That last week the whole family

had a bon voyage party for him. He sulked in a chair
by the pistachios, half-smiling for pictures.

From the long end of the pool table, I stared death
in the face, and realized we have the same grin.

Last night, I dreamt that I was pushing a plastic stroller
along Manton Avenue where my father used to smoke

joints and play football. He was the captain.
I wanted to take the baby to Grandpa's bar

where Dad used to do his dealing. I wanted to show
off his *extraordinary*, chronicled in all the poems

I haven't written. In my dream, I walked through
the smoked glass and my uncle was pouring drinks,

my cousin was sitting in a chair by the green nuts.
I looked around for my father.

I searched the bathrooms and the patio.
I looked under the cognac bottles where he used to

hide the white powder. I asked my uncle if he'd seen
my father. He bent his forehead into a V, told me

Your father is dead. I asked my cousin if it was true.
He pulled up his sleeve and showed me a memorial tattoo.

But eventually I found him,
I heard a voice familiar as teeth coming from

inside the carriage, where he'd been all along, blinking his eyes
at the fluorescent lights.

PETRARCHAN

The sonnet I most resemble is you.
I got a Roman candle in my crotch,
Bocce balls simmering in a sexpot.
Olive oil softens my tongue. I stole soot
From your hair and hid it in the long boot
Of my windpipe. This language is earmarked
By hand gestures adorned like bedposts notched
With Apollonia, rapt by a brute—
The truth is: I'm from canned marinara.
Mom uses no Rs, Dad's a wannabe
Gangsta. It's all the Italian I am.
My role model's a young John Travolta.
Still white like Maine. More apple than fig tree.
Eyes bluer than the Mediterranean.

CUTTING STEVENS

We were going to examine "The Snowman."
It was a literature seminar, and Wallace Stevens
was going to be cross-compared to the rapper
Young Jeezy, who dons a glittering snowman
on his chest. The snowman being the metaphor
for cocaine of course. The seminar was part
of the university's campaign to appeal to "urban"
students, and they named it *Lit-Hop*, and they hired
a snowflake, the son of a snow-dealer, to teach it.
It was a winter like Pluto. Pluto being the simile
for cold of course. The snow piled up like penguins
and sea lions, and many classes were canceled
that semester. To rectify, I had to cut lessons,
lop the hands off of poets, remove the icy watches
from rappers.

CONGO

In the Congo, the disc jockey has one hand.

On his left arm, just below his elbow
is a stub, dark and calloused like a stump,
he uses to cross fade the jam.

An eight-year-old boy with a rifle helps him
lift vinyl from a green crate, as bodies pogo up
and down like gazelles.

Because the rifle rules that dance floor, *The Jackson Five*
get played again and again and again.

In the Congo, young girls who speak Swahili, sing
I Get Around in perfect Tupac.

In the Congo, fuck "water from stone." Try blood
from mango. Try crucifix from white rhino.

Hey young world: Mobutu is wearing a leopard,
six feet below the earth, in box made of copper.
America is still the river that eats all rivers.

In America, the disc jockey has no hands.

A sixty-year-old man with a toupee and diamond
cuff links, below the elbows, presses the buttons
that cross fade the jam.

In America, Funk Master Flex is filled with cotton.
Angie Martinez has hooks in her shoulders, twine holding
her smile in place.

Hey young world: There are machetes in the airwaves,
cutting the wax that melts teen ears, to guava jelly.

Because the dollar rules this dance floor, the gunshot
gets played like buck buck buck.

ON TURNING 30

It was a spotless account—while the waiter poured wine—
Noel explained how her boyfriend's eyes just rolled back.
How his pulse went slack as she squeezed his wrist
like a flashlight, hoping the bulb would turn back on.
The mouth to mouth she gave him was nothing like on TV,
she said. There's all kinds of fluids, she said, and the face
changes color, she said, and the skin gets cold—because this
isn't acting, and there's no makeup. In the emergency room,
doctors pushed on his chest like an accordion trying to make
heart music. The blood volcanoed from his mouth,
painted the ceiling a rouge Pollock. There was no explanation
for this artistry. Science came up with nothing.
She talked about how every day farther from the tragedy
is more difficult because each day is one more day wedged
between her, and him alive. So really this pain—she doesn't
want it to pass with time. She wants time to paralyze,
so the photographs are only two weeks and eleven hours
before my birthday. The smiles still make sense.
On May 7th 2005, I think about how poetry isn't a way of writing,
but more a way of seeing. It took me thirty spins to come to this.
On a personal note, the wretched poem now looked like this:
Clean as a U-shaped yellow counter—while the waiter poured
wine—Noel goes on and on about the desperation in their final kiss.
The only thing I hear is: *only thirty and in perfect health.*
This makes me feel lightheaded, as we eat Taglierini Empolese
from my favorite little café, drink from long-stemmed glasses,
Valpolicella wine. All I can think of is myself.
How I don't want to die. Sweat beads along the rim of my upper lip.
I squirm in my seat.

ON TURNING 32

The mandate states that aging will happen once a year.
365¼ days accumulate all in one moment, and you're stuck
like that, till your next birthday. For me, the change occurs
on May 7th at 10:32:22 am.

Furthermore, all accomplishments, all disaster and folly
from the previous year, will register at the second you were born.
That is when all awards will be sealed. All losses calculated
on your flesh. It is recommended that you go about your days
without expectation. Go like a banana slug.

So when Jeremy welcomed his 21st year with a shot of good Scotch,
22 met him with fifteen new pounds, and a DUI. On Laura's 15th,
she became a new mom and joined the YMCA—108,000 sit-ups later,
her sweet 16 was magic, when in *one instant* loose flesh
turned metal. It was like watching a drip castle in reverse.

Larry, who was born at 3:22:43 am, went to bed anxious as a ferret
because of an early morning staff meeting, and woke up on July 22nd
bald as a turtle, with no job.

Many have learned to adjust to this style of aging, how everything
catches up in a moment. Samantha starved herself from February 6th
to March 6th, to no avail. Joseph went about his life's chores
like a Buddhist, and cashed in as he blew out the candles. Nancy
was a bit more Hendrix with hers, so when she turned 45, her children
were taken away. Yellow rings wormed around her eyes.

Some peoples' bank accounts doubled. Other folks just vanished.
This year, instead of opening gifts—my uncle, grandpa, grandmother
and father— all made love to oblivion when the clock struck.

On my 32nd birthday, I sat at my empty desk and watched my watch nervously. When the second hand swept over the exact second I was born—*poof*—a pile of papers appeared like high rises.

I transformed into a small black bird, and with that, flew out my office window. The papers rustled like feathers.

Waiting for Poems

Ever since my father's funeral, all my dead relatives
are lined up in the in-between waiting for their poems. They heard me recite
about heaven in front of his casket, and want a trope that shares shrimp cocktail
with God. I'm trying to scratch at the sacred in me that strings words together
like popcorn and cranberries. They don't understand these things take time.
But Uncle Jimmy's been dead for almost a year now.
He wants me to incorporate Chinese pugs and Harley Davidsons into his elegy.
Papa John prefers something more simple: seventeen truckers huddled over
coffee mugs, strips of bacon singing on the grill in tercets.
My grandmother would like a verse with airbrushed cheeks, smack on the cover
of a dime store novel. Grandpa Vin needs a ten-gallon hat and a poker table
surrounded by all of his buddies—with mouths like greyhounds—in his metaphor.
Meanwhile dad is not satisfied with the poem he got. He wants 14 *more* lines,
one final couplet that paints him in that soft forgiving light.

ACKNOWLEDGMENTS:

Grateful acknowledgment is made to the editors of the following publications where these poems first appeared:

Get Underground: "Graffiti"
Hanging Loose: "Congo," "Dancing with Turtle," "Dead Ass," "Lobster with Ol' Dirty Bastard," "Zev Love X Live at His Brother's Funeral"
National Poetry Slam Anthology: High Desert Voices: "Losing Creativity"
New York Quarterly: "Crossing Brooklyn Bridge," "Dearest Workshop"
November 3rd Club: "Congo"
Perillo Prize Finalist: "Waiting for Poems"
Spindle Magazine: "Revolution Concerts," "The Message"
Spoken Word Revolution Redux (Vol. 2): "Dead Ass"
Texas Review: "On Turning 30"
Word Is Bond: "Culture"
World Literature Today; "Best Use for My Poems"

The poems "Balloon," "Embrace," "Kissing Turtles," "Sher-Holder," and "You Were Wearing" first appeared in the illustrated anthology *The Last American Valentine* (Write Bloody, 2008).

"Love Song for Kelis" was featured on *HBO's Def Poetry* (Season 5).

This book is also indebted to the support, friendship and counsel of Erica Miriam Fabri, without whom my work wouldn't be what it is. Your poetry is an inspiration, your guidance is impeccable. Thank you.

Huge thanks to the folks who have been my friends and poetic mentors, formally and informally: David Lehman, Elaine Equi, Patricia Smith, Bob Holman, Jeffrey McDaniel, Willie Perdomo, Prageeta Sharma, both Rachels (Kann & RAC, and Holden, Pipe and Clem), Celena Glenn & Bunny, April, Queen GodIs, K~Swift, Derrick Brown, Beau Sia, Christa Bell, Geoff & Em, Jessica, Aracelis Girmay, my New School cohort, PEN Center West, Italian American Writers' Association, the Bowery Poetry Club and Gary Glazner, louderArts and Bar 13 and Maureen, and everyone from my poetry slam communities in Oakland and The Bay, Long Beach and NYC. To too many friends to name, you're my heart. Thank you to the emcees and groups—especially Trugoy, Lupe Fiasco, Black Star, The Roots, Pharoahe Monch, Kanye West, and Sage Francis—who inspired my work. I am a fan.

Forever thanks to Hanging Loose Press, and my meticulous editors Donna Brook and Bob Hershon. Forever and ever thanks to Urban Word NYC for giving my life purpose, ambition and joy. Thank you to all the UW mentors for making this org tick so precisely and beautifully. Thank you to Jen Weiss, Parker, Shaun, Lisa, Marc, Marissa, Tahani and the Word Wide Youth Leadership Board, Marty McConnell and Tracy Meade. FBIII, AfroKen, Nisa, Naz & D, holla! Erin and Babycakes. Willy Ney, the University of Wisconsin, Anna West and NYSWC. Alan Sitomer for the opportunities, friendship and future! Allison for the cover, the friendship, and Puba 2000!

Love and thanks to the Cirelli family, Michael Cirelli for this final gift, and my grandparents Donna and Vincent Cirelli. All my love to my little-sister-poet-in-the-wings Amber, and my one and only Nana.

Love and gratitude to Sara for the patience and the love. I love you.

To my parents Joseph and Patricia Mangione, I hope that one day I will be skilled enough to write something that is worthy of you. You are my heroes.